Have Fun!
— Cianna

Enjoy!
— Iqbal

The opinions expressed in this manuscript are solely the opinions of the author and do not represent the opinions or thoughts of the publisher. The author has represented and warranted full ownership and/or legal right to publish all the materials in this book.

LAS VEGAS ... ARE WE THERE YET?
A Book by Kids From Las Vegas (and Their Parents, Too!)
All Rights Reserved.
Copyright © 2014 Izobel, Cianna, Debbie & Peter Sturges
v2.0 r1.0

This book may not be reproduced, transmitted, or stored in whole or in part by any means, including graphic, electronic, or mechanical without the express written consent of the publisher except in the case of brief quotations embodied in critical articles and reviews.

Outskirts Press, Inc.
http://www.outskirtspress.com

ISBN: 978-1-4787-0021-0

Outskirts Press and the "OP" logo are trademarks belonging to Outskirts Press, Inc.

PRINTED IN THE UNITED STATES OF AMERICA

Do you want to have some fun? Check us out... Las Vegas is the place to be! We have so many things happening here for families and kids! Beat the summer heat with a new water park called Wet 'n' Wild. It is awesome! During winter, I love going to the Magical Forest and sledding in the snow at Mt. Charleston. There's a lot to do here, so please read our book and see why you should plan your next vacation to Las Vegas. You'll really have a great time!

— Izobel S.

Our city is FA-BU-LOUS!!! That's what our famous sign says: Welcome to Fabulous Las Vegas. Yes, it's totally true! So many of our family and friends from other states and other countries are always excited to visit us here. When they come, I like to go with them to the Strip. I love the Dancing Fountains, the Atlantis Show, the Fremont Street Experience, and many more! Come see our fabulous city!

— Cianna

DEAR FAMILY TRAVELERS,
   This book is your key to orchestrating your itinerary and micro managing your trip to one of the world's most popular destinations... LAS VEGAS!
   For those unfamiliar with this neon oasis, you are in for a treat! So you think Las Vegas is only about casinos? Think again! You won't believe what family-friendly gems there are in the city. Las Vegas offers the unexpected - it's bursting at the seams with wholesome family entertainment - seriously, there is never enough time to see and do them all!
   After more than 10 years of showing off our city to visitors, we have compiled some savvy suggestions for you to check out. Browse through our sample itinerary so you can concoct a schedule that can keep kids blissfully occupied and adults gloriously pampered. Best of all, we created a one-of-a-kind memory keepsake for the children to journal their experiences and showcase their fave pictures.
   So, c'mon....! Embark on a learning holiday adventure! Ramp up the fun!!! Broaden your children's worldview! Dazzle them...! Stoke their interest!!! MAKE THIS A VACATION YOU'LL ALL REMEMBER FOREVER!!!

DEBBI (MOM)

KNOWN WORLD-WIDE, LAS VEGAS IS A CITY LIKE NO OTHER!
DOCUMENT YOUR ADVENTURE WITH OUR HELPFUL GUIDE, AND SHARE YOUR BRAG BOOK WITH FRIENDS AND FAMILY... ENJOY!
PETER (DAD)

Contents

Introduction iii
Acknowledgments vi
Advisory & Disclaimer vi
F.Y.I. 1

Las Vegas Family Travel Information
   1. Free Attractions 6
      Mom's & Dad's Top Suggestions ... To Free Attractions ... 7
   2. Free Entertainment 8
      Mom's & Dad's Top Suggestions ... To Free Entertainment ... 9
   3. Swimming & Pool Fun 10
      Mom's & Dad's Top Suggestions ... To Swimming & Pool Fun ... 11
   4. Amusement Parks & Rides 12
      Mom's & Dad's Top Suggestions ... Amusement Parks & Rides ... 13
   5. The Great Outdoors 14
      Mom's & Dad's Top Suggestions ... To The Great Outdoors ... 15
   6. Food & Dining 16
      Mom's & Dad's Top Suggestions ... To Food & Dining ... 17
   7. Shopping & Malls 18
      Mom's & Dad's Top Suggestions ... To Shopping & Malls ... 19
   8. Shows, Magic, & Circus Acts 20
      Mom's & Dad's Top Suggestions ... To Shows, Magic, & Circus Acts ... 21
   9. Museums, Arts, & Arcades 22
      Mom's & Dad's Top Suggestions ... To Museums, Art, & Arcades ... 23
  10. Other Fun Stuff 24
      Mom's & Dad's Top Suggestions ... To Other Fun Stuff ... 25

Extra Features
   1. Map of Las Vegas 27
   2. Travel Budget Checklist 28
   3. Packing List 1: For kids/teens 29
   4. Packing List 2: For parents/adults 31
   5. Sample Itinerary 33
   6. Other Resources 39

BONUS!! My Travel Brag Book (Journal & Photo Souvenir) 41

ACKNOWLEDGMENTS

This book would not have been possible without the sincere help and collective effort of a wonderful team at Outskirts Press. Special thanks to Larry S. Gray, our Publishing Consultant, for his wisdom and extreme patience; Jodee Thayer, the Director of Author Services, for her valuable advices and suggestions; the phenomenal Production Team - Bridget Horstmann and Rebecca Andreas; and our Graphic Designer, for turning this undeveloped project into a stunning reality.

ADVISORY & DISCLAIMER

Travel information, prices, and schedule of events, can change unexpectedly. We strongly advise that you write or call ahead for confirmation when making your travel plans. Every effort has been made to ensure the accuracy of information throughout this book, and the contents of this publication are believed correct at the time of printing. Assessments of places and events are based upon the authors' own experience, and descriptions in this book may contain an element of subjective opinion. Nevertheless, the authors, editors, and publisher cannot be held responsible for inaccuracies, errors, omissions, or changes in details given in this guide, or for the consequences of information, inconvenience, loss, damage, costs, expenses incurred or suffered, and experiences of readers while traveling. Any mention of a name of a company, organization, or website in this guide, does not mean that we endorse them. Be aware that information provided through some websites may be unreliable and can change without notice. Neither the publisher nor authors shall be liable for any damages arising from the same. Your safety is important to us, and we encourage you to stay alert and be aware of your surroundings. Keep your children close by at all times and keep a close eye on cameras, purses, wallets, valuables, and all favorite targets of thieves and pickpockets.

There are so much more wonderful places, events, and activities that you might have discovered and you would like to share with your fellow travelers. Please write to:

www.outskirtspress.com/LasVegasarewethereyet?

F.Y.I.

Did you know "Las Vegas" is Spanish for "The Meadows"? That was the name given by explorers in 1829 when they discovered the valley full of lush greenery and springs.

"Las Vegas" and "Vegas" are one and the same city. Lots of people just like to fondly shorten it. Not like New York, you can't just say "York," or San Diego, just "Diego... awkward, huh?

Oh, if you hear everyone saying "The Strip," it doesn't mean you have to strip your clothes... duhhh!!! It refers to the long, straight street called Las Vegas Boulevard where all the gigantic hotels are.

When you hear about "Downtown," it's where the older and original hotels are. The famous, dazzling eye-popping "Fremont Street Experience" is also found Downtown.

1

According to the U.S. Census Bureau, the estimated population of the Las Vegas in 2011 was 589,317 and 2,770,028 for Nevada.
(http://quickfacts.census.gov/qfd/states/32000.html)

And guess how many tourists visit Las Vegas each year? Around 40 million! Isn't that mind-boggling?

Everyone thinks Las Vegas is mostly for adults because of the casinos, gambling places, and some age-inappropriate shows. But there are tons of shows that are good for family and kids, too! Lots of amazing Magic shows... yessss!

And did we say that parking is free in most hotels? Our visitors are always amazed by this. Cool, right?

Warning: There is curfew for those under 18 years old on the Strip and any other public places - they are not allowed out alone during the following hours:

	School Season	School Holidays & Summer Vacation
Sun - Thurs	10pm to 5am	Midnight to 5am
Fri - Sat	Midnight to 5am	Midnight to 5am
Fri-Sat (The Strip)	9pm-5am	9pm-5am

(ref: Clark County Municipal Code Title: 12.12).

Have you ever seen a city with a lot of cute wedding chapels? Only in Las Vegas! Some also say that Las Vegas is the Wedding Capital of the World.

Please wear comfy shoes! Our hotels are colossal, like, almost Titanic huge! You will easily get tired walking those miles. Don't forget to bring snacks, too. Long strolls in the hotels can be energy-draining... take it from me!

Do you know who Elvis Presley is? You can see a lot of him here, even if the original one is long gone and up in heaven. There are many famous celebrities in Vegas - our city is full of stars!

Advance travel learning tip: Read about the Pyramid, Sphinx, Obelisk (Egypt), the Eiffel Tower (Paris), the Roman Empire especially about Julius Caesar, Legends of King Arthur and his court during the Medieval times, Gondolas (Venice), the Statue of Liberty, and more... You will see them all here! Uh... replicas of the real ones, yes ☺

Another warning: Youngsters and babies are not allowed in the casinos, except when just passing through, and with an adult – not roaming around unattended. Period.

Our summers are super hot, so hydrate, hydrate, hydrate! Carry a water bottle with you at all times.

It is advisable to call beforehand to check the hotels, and confirm events, activities, etc... that you would like to go to because Vegas is such a hectic place, changes happen as fast as you blink your eye!

Did you know that Las Vegas is the Number 1 Trade Show Destination in the U.S.? So when you plan your trip, make sure to check that there is no important convention, or else your rates will be high, and traffic will be crazy!

There are reasons why Las Vegas is the "Entertainment Capital of the World"... and you are about to discover them!!! Read on...

1. FREE ATTRACTIONS
Here are our awesome ideas!!!

Bellagio Hotel
3600 Las Vegas Blvd S
888-987-6667

Largest Chocolate Fountain
Season-changing Conservatory &
Botanical Gardens
Dancing Fountains

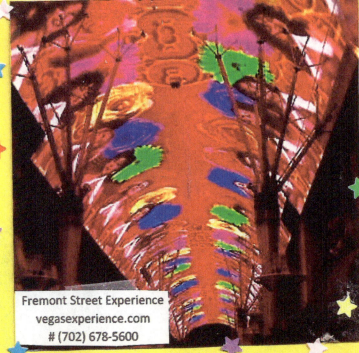

Fremont Street Experience
vegasexperience.com
(702) 678-5600

MOM'S & DAD'S TOP SUGGESTIONS ... TO FREE ATTRACTIONS.

No other city has freebies-galore like Las Vegas! Mastermind your itineraries to include these jaw-dropping "free-of-charge" attractions in the city. With astute, sensible, and sticking to wallet-friendly activities, you will have a Vegas experience like no other!

The Las Vegas Welcome Sign – a must-see for first-timers! This iconic sign on the south edge of the Strip is a blazing riot of colorful splendor - its flashy and flamboyant design aptly represents the opulent city to a tee! Don't. miss. this!

Wildlife Habitat, Flamingo Hotel, 3555 Las Vegas Blvd. Meander through this 15-acre lush habitat (open 24/7) which is home to flamingos, penguins, birds, cranes, swans, fishes and others. For a more intimate experience, schedule your visit when the flamingos are fed daily. Check timings. Tel # (702) 733-3111

Chocolate lovers ... celebrate! You are in Chocolate Paradise! There's no skimping on this aphrodisiac with 3 sinfully indulgent locations within a stone's throw away from each other. Besides gawking at the **largest chocolate waterfall at the Bellagio Hotel,** wallow in 4 stories of seizure-inducing chocolate madness at **M&M's World**, Showcase Mall, 3785 Las Vegas Blvd. Still can't get enough of chocolate? Make a beeline for **Hershey's Chocolate World** (opening winter 2013) at the New York-New York Hotel, 3790 Las Vegas Blvd. The visits are free. Resisting the temptation? Priceless!

World of Coca-Cola. You can't miss the gigantic bottle looming next to MGM Grand, 3785 Las Vegas Blvd. This building is packed with endless display of ... you guess it right, Coca-cola memorabilia and collectibles!

Free tram rides. A network of panoramic, enjoyable and accessible rides connects various hotels: Excalibur-Luxor-Mandalay Bay, T.I.-Mirage, Monte Carlo-Aria-Vdara-City Center-Bellagio. These rides never fail to fascinate kids. Simple pleasures!

MOM'S & DAD'S TOP SUGGESTIONS ... TO FREE ENTERTAINMENT.

Die-hard show lovers will get a kick out of bragging to friends back home that they've watched world-class shows in Las Vegas for a seductive price of ... how much? ZERO!!! Yes, an exciting collection of extraordinary and captivating shows await everyone, like:

Erupting Volcano at the Mirage, 3400 Las Vegas Blvd. This realistic and spectacular nightly thunderous show is simply mind-blowing! Call Tel # 800-374-9000 to inquire for the "erupting" schedules.

Lake of Dreams, Wynn Hotel, 3131 Las Vegas Blvd. Desire to be transported to a mystical world? Then grab a strategic viewing area to watch this dazzling and breathtaking light and water show. Dial Tel # (702) 770-3392 and be mesmerized!

Blue Man Group, Monte Carlo Hotel, 3770 Las Vegas Blvd. Catch the teaser procession before the electrifying nightly show. *"Each night the Blue Men deliver an extraordinary spectacle as well as a soulful and primal kind of euphoric experience that makes you feel vibrantly alive and more closely connected with the people around you"*. Quoted from www.montecarlo.com/ entertainment/bluemangroup Tel # 888-529-4828

Fountain Show and Rainstorm, Planet Hollywood, 3663 Las Vegas Blvd. Two heart-pounding events await you in the Miracle Mile Shops. Don't miss the bursts of light, water effects, and color-changing fog at the Fountain, and the lightning, thunder, and rainstorm at the mini harbor. Call Tel # (702) 866-0710 for show times.

When strolling down the Strip after dusk, catch the **colorful light, water, & sound** extravaganza at the entrance of **Bally's Hotel**, 3645 Las Vegas Blvd S. (702) 739-4111. Want to surprise your young kids and meet a "talking cow"? Schedule a free tour (and ice cream!) at the **Anderson Dairy** and see how dairy products are processed. (702) 642 7507 X 264. Highly informational! Here's a sneak peak: http://www.andersondairy.com/barnyardtour.php. Elvis fans check this out! Don't miss the longest running Elvis Presley tribute show by Pete **"Big Elvis"** Vallee at Harrah's Piano Bar, 3475 Las Vegas Blvd S. Free admission. (702) 369-5000.

MOM'S & DAD'S TOP SUGGESTIONS ...
TO SWIMMING & POOL FUN.

Let the Funshine begin!!! A much-awaited incredible water park made a splashy debut during the summer of 2013 - it is quenching the excitement of water-lovers and thrill-seekers alike! **Wet'n'Wild**. The pinnacle of summer fun! The name itself evokes unbridled freedom. Plunge into their more than 25 thrill slides and amazing water attractions ... and unleash your untamed spirit!

Check out the fantastic features at www.wetnwildlasvegas.com *"Adrenaline junkies can enjoy ride experiences like the Hoover Half Pipe, that drops you a gut-wrenching 57 feet into a giant half pipe, or the raging Rattler, the only slide of its kind in North America. The park also features family-friendly attractions such as the relaxing Colorado Cooler, a 1,000-foot-long winding lazy river; Splash Island, a multi-level interactive children's area filled with geysers, mini-slides and dumping buckets; and the giant wave pool, Red Rock Bay".* Tel # (702) 979-1600

Another "fun-tastic" park is scheduled to open in 2014. Beat the heat at **Cowabunga Bay**. Summers will never be the same in Las Vegas! www.cowabungabay.com

Ramp up the water fun and soak up some sun and some sand in this selection of top picks - you will be amazed at what hotel pools offer!

- Tropical lazy river and incredibly enjoyable wave pool at **Mandalay Bay.**
- Water slide and alluring waterfalls at **Flamingo Hotel**.
- Exotic lagoon and lush surroundings at the **Mirage**.
- Majestic Garden of the Gods Oasis at **Caesar's Palace**.
- A long and winding lazy river and 5 engaging pools at the **MGM Grand**.
- Cascading falls and shady scenic palm trees at the **Tropicana Hotel**.
- Waterfall and gazebo area for sun-worshippers at the **South Point.**
- Oversized, outdoor tropical swimming pool oasis at **Blu Pool, Bally's**
- One-of-a-kind "Swim with the Sharks" Aquarium with falls, a wild 3-story slide for families at The Tank, and an Infinity pool for ages 16 and over, **Golden Nugget.**

NOTES

_____
_____
_____
_____
_____
_____

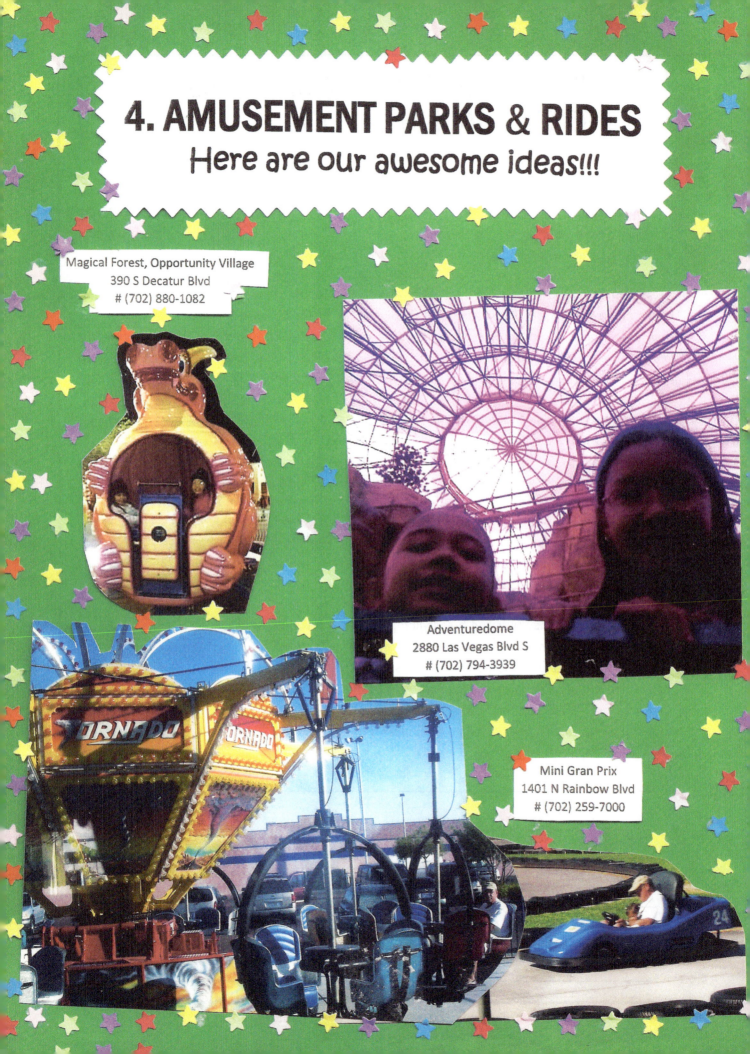

MOM'S & DAD'S TOP SUGGESTIONS ... AMUSEMENT PARKS & RIDES

Ready to let your exuberant and bouncy children burn off their excess energy? The requirements: Adrenaline rush. Check. Heart-pounding gasps. Check. Gut-wrenching screams. Check. All these in Las Vegas? Check. Here's where to bring the older kids and teens ... and let loose!!!

Feel your heart stop! The 360 degrees stunning view of the city is drown out by sheer terror of the 4 extreme thrill rides: **SkyJump, Big Shot, X Scream, and Insanity**, on the top of the 900 ft high **Stratosphere Tower**, 2000 Las Vegas Blvd. Tel # (702) 380-7777. Wild. Like, totally!

Take an exhilarating ride on the **Manhattan Express Roller Coaster** that will "*lift you up 203 feet, drop you down 144 feet and leave your pulse trying to catch up*" as per lasvegas.com. Tel # (702)740-6969 **New York-New York** 3790 Las Vegas Blvd.

Zip through a heart-pumping adventure beneath a blast of kaleidoscopic light show at the Fremont Experience. **Flightlinez** will make your Downtown experience truly unforgettable! 425 Fremont Street. Tel # (702) 410-7999

The ultimate thrill of a lifetime! **Vegas Indoor Skydiving** Tel # 877-545-8093 "*Experience bodyflight similar to the "freefall aspect of skydiving without the use of airplane or parachute*" and earn your wings! Reference: www.vegasindoorskydiving.com

Fulfill your dreams! Drive exotic cars! Moms and Dads can cross this off their bucket lists. Check out **World Class Driving** Tel # 877-597-6403, or simply drive Dream cars and Luxury vehicles from the airport through Hertz, Avis, and Enterprise Rent-a-Car. How about heavy equipment like excavators or bulldozers? Call **Dig This** at Tel # (702) 222-4344

Do you just want to go slow mo? For those who prefer a leisurely ride, enjoy a graceful glide down the **Grand Canal** in an authentic **gondola** at the **Venetian** and shhhh ... what's that? Opera??? Surprise! You will be serenaded by a melodious singing Gondolier! Advanced reservation strongly advised. Tel # (702) 414-3400.

NOTES

5. THE GREAT OUTDOORS
Here are our awesome ideas!!!

Local Parks
Clark County Parks & Recreation
(702) 455-8200

Mt. Charleston

Golfing

MOM'S & DAD'S TOP SUGGESTIONS ... TO THE GREAT OUTDOORS

Not to burst your bubble, but there's more to Las Vegas than just the glitzy casinos. Oh, yes! With more than 360 days of invigorating sunshine, our city boasts of a deep sun-kissed landscape and rich lush desert environment. A first-time visitor gets slammed with the unexpected: a concrete jungle and throbbing metropolis teeming with frenetic tourists! But ... cast your eyes beyond the outlandish architecture and you will be taken aback to discover that Las Vegas snugly nestles in a deep valley surrounded by the majestic Spring Mountains. The city is a magical blend of the urban and the natural beauty!

Escape the euphoria of the neon-soaked city, just 15 miles west, to a panorama that transports you beyond the familiar, and into the sublime. **Red Rock Canyon.** Here's where you can commune with nature and get transfixed by the multicolor boulders, stimulating hiking trails and a scenic loop drive. Tel. # (702) 515-5367

Explore a quaint, authentic western town called **Bonnie Springs Ranch,** Blue Diamond Road. There you will find a museum, cowboy shows, a saloon, a petting zoo, horseback riding, and more. Tel # (702) 875-4191 www.bonniesprings.com

Drive further northeast and camp, picnic, or hike at the breathtaking, loaded with vibrant vistas **Valley of Fire State Park,** Overton Tel # (702) 397-2088

Do you know that we have the "*largest water reservoir in the U.S. in maximum water capacity?*" Reference: en.wikipedia.org/wiki/lakemead. The picturesque **Lake Mead** offers year-round boating, fishing, picnicking, and more. Tel # (702)293-8990

Expand your horizon and head 31 miles southeast of Las Vegas, to an architectural marvel that will dumbfound you. The world-famous **Hoover Dam** is a hydroelectric power plant named after the 31st President of America, Herbert Hoover. This must-see wonder is the highest dam in the U.S. Tel # 866-730-9097.

MOM'S & DAD'S TOP SUGGESTIONS ... TO FOOD & DINING

Eat like Royalty! Las Vegas is the ultimate food lovers' paradise. With a wide range of elegant restaurants, chick eateries, bistros and gut-busting buffets that give your eyes as much pleasure as your taste buds, all of your favorites are here ... and more! This glitzy city has elevated dining to meteoric levels!

Take a culinary adventure in **The Walking Gourmet** Food Tours, a *"food tasting exploration of the many eclectic tastes of Las Vegas"* reference: www.thewalkinggourment.com. Tel # (702) 2211-1958. Incomparable!

Nothing screams gluttony like a buffet, but 6 buffets in 24 hours? Only in Las Vegas can you fulfill your gastronomic fantasies with **Buffet of Buffets**! Work out a gargantuan appetite and check out more information at www.TotalLV.com Bon Appétit!

Buffets are convenient when you have kids in tow, but due to its popularity, lines can be stressfully long and exorbitant prices can be migraine-inducing. Still, find out why everyone's raving about the **Wicked Spoon**, Cosmopolitan. # (702) 698-7000, Buffets at **Aria** # (702) 230-2742, **Bellagio** # (702) 693-8111, **Wynn** # (702) 770-3340, **Green Valley Ranch** # (702) 617-7777, **Bacchanal** at Caesar's Palace # (702) 731-7110, and **Carnival World Buffet**, Rio # (702) 777-7777.

Finally, soak your palate in a smorgasbord of **Celebrity Chefs'** restaurants that cluster in every corner of the city. As icing on the cake, we'll throw in some formidable names:

Alain Ducasse
Bradley Ogden
David Myers
Emeril Lagasse
Gordon Ramsay
Jean Joho
Jose Andres
Laurent Tourondel
Masa Takayama
Nobu Matsuhisa
Paul Bartolotta
Shawn McClain
Tom Moloney

Andre Rochat
Carla Pellegrino
David Walzog
Fiorenzo Trunzo
Hubbert Keller
Jean Philippe
Julian Serrano
Luciano Pellegrini
Michael Mina
Piero Selvaggio
Rick Moonen
Todd English
Wolfgang Puck

Bobby Flay
Charlie Palmer
Eric Bromberg
Francois Payard
Jean Georges
Joel Robuchon
Kerry Simon
Mario Batali
Michel Richard
Pierre Gagnaire
Scott Conant
Tom Collichio
and more to come...

NOTES

_____
_____
_____
_____
_____
_____

MOM'S & DAD'S TOP SUGGESTIONS ... TO SHOPPING & MALLS

You want it all!!! Just when you thought you held a tight grip on your purses, the tempting shops beckon. From the exquisite, to the whimsical, to the ultramodern - the impulse to treasure-trove the assortment of shops for an unparalleled shopping experience is irresistible. Shopaholics ... beware!!! A myriad of malls can more than satiate your shopping hysteria in Las Vegas. Giddying!

Start with the luxurious **Fashion Show Mall** "*at the edge of fashion, in the heart of Vegas*" reference: www.thefashionshow.com for an ultimate experience in shopping, dining, and entertainment. Tel # (702) 369-8382

Then, work your way to the uber-upscale **Crystals** at City Center # (702) 590-9299, where what you see will take your breath away, and where the kids will be entranced by Halo, a cutting-edge water display of swirling whirlpools, accented by colorful lights in clear canisters protruding from the floor. Futuristic!

Alternatively, rendezvous at these stylish hotel shops:
- The elegant **Esplanade** at the Wynn and Encore # (702) 770-7000
- The magnificent **Forum Shops** at Caesar's Palace # (702) 893-4800
- The fashionable **Grand Canal Shoppes** at the Venetian # (702) 414-4500
- The chic **Le Boulevard Shops** at the Paris, Las Vegas # (702) 946-7000
- The hip and trendy **LVH Shops** at the Las Vegas Hotel # (702) 732-5111
- The posh **Miracle Mile Shops** at Planet Hollywood # (702) 866-0703
- The classy **Mandalay Place** at Mandalay Bay # (702) 632-7777
- The sophisticated **Via Bellagio** at the Bellagio # (702) 693-7111

And finally, casually stroll through these cozy, open-air, family-friendly, Village-atmosphere malls with dedicated play areas for children:
- The charming **Tivoli Village** # (702) 570-7400
- The vibrant **Town Square** # (702) 269-5000
- The impressionable **District at Green Valley Ranch** # (702) 564-8595

MOM'S & DAD'S TOP SUGGESTIONS ...
TO SHOWS, MAGIC, & CIRCUS ACTS

Really? Still think Vegas is not family-friendly? Browse through the extensive list of shows in the city and this page cannot accommodate the number of entertainment geared towards families and kids. Don't leave Vegas without watching one of these buzz-worthy shows!

Let's start with the World's most popular illusionist, Guinness World of Records holder, Emmy Award Winner, *Living Legend* (named by the US Library of Congress) and Master Magician **David Copperfield**. Mind-blowing! Watch him bring real magic to life at the MGM Grand. www.davidcopperfield.com

Hopscotch down the block to Luxor Hotel and be mystified by the most watched magician in Internet history Criss Angel in his Cirque du Soleil show "*BeLIEve*" www.crissangel.com

Work your way up the Strip to Planet Hollywood for these amazing shows: **Nathan Burton** Magic and Comedy www.nathanburton.com; **Gerry McCambridge** with mind reading and seemingly psychic powers www.TheMentalist.com; and the "*most beloved family show in the world*" **Popovich Comedy Pet Theater,** featuring extraordinary, talented, and incredible performing cats, dogs, and parrots www.comedypet.com.

Catch **Jan Rouven's** Illusions Show at the Riviera and see why he was Voted Best Magician by a Reader's Poll 2013 for the Las Vegas Review Journal www.janrouven.com.

Magic Castle in Hollywood named **Mac King** "*Magician of the Year*". This hilarious performer has an array of magic tricks at Harrahs Hotel. www.mackingshow.com.

Puppets!! Re-introduce the children to the world of ventriloquism in **Terry Fator's** Show at the Mirage. He was voted Best Impressionist by Las Vegas Weekly www.terryfator.com.

How about transporting your eager children to the land of jousting, sword fights, horses, knights, beautiful dancing maidens, and everything Medieval? **Tournament of Kings** Dinner Show will simply entrance them! www.Excalibur.com/TournamentofKings

9. MUSEUMS, ARTS, & ARCADES
Here are our awesome ideas!!!

Madame Tussauds
3377 Las Vegas Blvd S
(702) 862-7800

Discovery Children's Museum
360 Promenade Pl
(702) 382-5437

First Friday
1228 S Casino Center

MOM'S & DAD'S TOP SUGGESTIONS ...
TO MUSEUMS, ART, & ARCADES

Ramp up the learning experience of your bright-eyed and enthusiastic kids in the city's fertile arsenal of "one-of-a-kind" resources. What's quirky is that these off-beat places can be insanely fun, too!

Let the children explore the interactive **Springs Preserve** at 333 S. Valley View Blvd www.springspreserve.org

Venture into the world of sharks, Komodo dragon, sawfish, piranhas, giant rays, and more, at the **Shark Reef Aquarium**, Mandalay Bay www.sharkreef.com

Step into a different dimension in the **Neon Museum and Boneyard** which is reminiscent of the old Las Vegas where original signs are preserved and exhibited at 770 N Las Vegas Blvd www.neonmuseum.org

Two very informational exhibitions at the Luxor can be mesmerizing: **Bodies - The Exhibition and Titanic: The Artifact Exhibition.**

While the lively arts scene of the city is showcased by the **First Friday** in the **Downtown area** every month (picture on the left), the cultural scene is bolstered by the magnificent **Smith Center for Performing Arts -** the citadel of arts in Las Vegas, 361 Symphony Park Ave. www.thesmithcenter.com Tel. (702) 749-2012

If you want to incorporate a trip to a state-of-the-art Arcade, check out:

    Gameworks next to MGM Grand
    Midway Arcade at Circus Circus
    Coney Island Emporium Arcade at New York-New York
    Strat-o-fair Arcade at Stratosphere
    Wizard's Arcade/Fantasy Faire Midway & **Fun Dungeon** at the Excalibur

Ok go ahead ... gasp! Yes, there's more, but we're space-challenged, so follow the droves of tourists and they will lead you to the fun zones!!!

MOM'S & DAD'S TOP SUGGESTIONS ... TO OTHER FUN STUFF

When you say Las Vegas, does anyone even conjure up images of snowboarding, auto racing, skydiving, boating, ballooning, horseback riding, or ice skating? Naaahh ... Well, we've got news for you! Our eclectic city has all these ... and more!!!

And get this. What city has the most **Cirque du Soleil Shows,** 9 as of this writing in 2013? You got it ... only in Las Vegas!

Moving on to under-the-radar experiences ... have a one-on-one with the King of the Jungle at the **Lion Habitat Ranch** # (702) 595-6666. Go aquatic and check out the dolphins in the **Secret Garden and Dolphin Habitat at the Mirage** # (800) 963-9634. Take a sweet tour of the **Ethel M Chocolate Factory and Cactus Gardens** # (702) 435-2655. Soar 400 feet above the Strip and dare to zip ride the **VooDoo Skyline** from one tower to another at the Rio! www.voodooskyline.com. Watch out for **SkyVue Super Wheel**, a giant Ferris wheel currently under construction in 2013 at the south end of the Strip, and the **Linq**, an open air retail, dining, and entertainment district, and its centerpiece, the **High Roller**, the tallest Observation Wheel in the World. At 550 feet tall, it is taller than the London Eye and Singapore flyer. **WOW!** www.caesars.com/thelinq

For **Golf** aficionado dads: Check out a world-class Tom Fazio 18-hole magnificent golf course right in the middle of the Strip! You do not even have to check in at the **Wynn or Encore** to play. Call # (702) 770-4653 for advance reservations. Otherwise, take a pick of the 61 golf courses in the city. You read it right ... 61 astonishing golf courses!

Other choices of unique glow-in-the dark mini-golf places besides King Putt that Izobel & Cianna suggested on the previous page are: **KISS**, # (702) 558-6256 www.monsterminigolf.com/KISS, **The Putt Park** www.theputtpark.com # (702) 254-7888, **3d Mini Golf** # (702) 608-4653, and **Pikes Pass**, inside Adventuredome # (702) 436-4653.

Oh, know something creepy? We do have **Ghost towns** here in Nevada! Spooky!

Or, take a drive to the desolate **Area 51**. Wikipedia says it is also known as "*Dreamland*, or "*Groom Lake*". What do you know about this mysterious stretch?

There's so much more! Just beyond the borders of Nevada and within easy driving distances, are stunning natural wonders: **Bryce Canyon** and **Zion National Park, Utah**; Death **Valley, California**; and the world-famous magnificent **Grand Canyon, Arizona**.

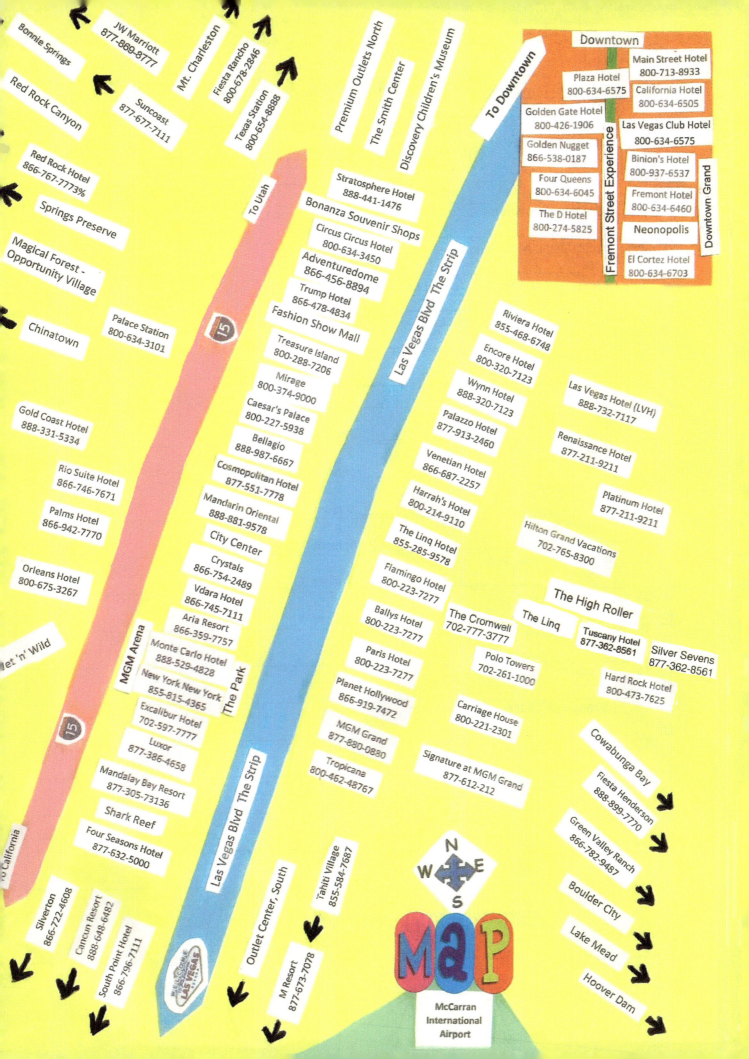

EXTRA FEATURE 2

TRAVEL BUDGET CHECKLIST
(Synchronize with Itinerary, Extra Feature 5)

#	ACTIVITY	AMOUNT
1	Airfare/or Gasoline budget for long car drive/cruising around $ _____ X _____ persons	
2	Hotel/Motel/Accommodation $ _____ X _____ days	
3	Car rental/transportation/or taxi expenses if not renting a car $ _____ X _____ days	
4	Fast food/casual meals/drinks/snacks $ _____ X _____ days	
5	Fine dining/Buffets $ _____ X _____ persons X _____ restaurants	
6	Childcare/babysitting services $ _____ X _____ days	
7	Tickets – family shows $ _____ X _____ persons X _____ shows	
8	Tickets – adult shows $ _____ X _____ persons X _____ shows	
9	Museums/Galleries $ _____ X _____ persons X _____ places	
10	Amusement park fees $ _____ X _____ persons X _____ places	
11	Package tours $ _____ X _____ persons X _____ tours	
12	Rides, Arcades	
13	Shopping – souvenirs	
14	Shopping – clothes, electronics, etc …	
15	Tips	
16		
17		
18		
	ESTIMATED TOTAL EXPENSES	

EXTRA FEATURE 3

CHILD/TEEN (1) PACKING LIST

	ITEM/S	Check before departure from	
		Home	Hotel
A.	**CARRY-ON**		
1	iPad/ipod/MP3/Music gadget		
2	Portable DVD/Electronic games/DSI/PSP etc …		
3	Travel-size board game/s		
4	1 comfort toy		
5	Books/crayons/pens/note pads		
6	Bag of dry snacks		
7	Travel-size wipes/tissues/hand sanitizer/lip balm		
8	Chewing gum/Ear plugs (to relieve air pressure during flight take off and landing)		
9	1 set extra clothes (in case luggage gets lost or misplaced)		
10			
11			
12			
13			
14			
B.	**LUGGAGE/CHECK-IN BAGGAGE**		
1	Season-appropriate clothes		
2	Swimwear for summer		
3	Jacket/sweater for winter		
4	Pouch for toiletries: comb, toothbrush, toothpaste, shampoo		
5	Blankie (if needed)		
6	Sleepwear, underwear, socks		
7	Shoes (_____ pairs), flip flops		
8	1 set semi-formal attire if planning to go for formal dinner/show		
9			
10			
11			
12			
13			
14			
TOTAL NUMBER OF PIECES OF LUGGAGE FOR CHILD/TEEN 1			

CHILD/TEEN (2) PACKING LIST

ITEM/S	Check before departure from	
	Home	Hotel
A. CARRY-ON		
1 iPad/ipod/MP3/Music gadget		
2 Portable DVD/Electronic games/DSI/PSP etc …		
3 Travel-size board game/s		
4 1 comfort toy		
5 Books/crayons/pens/note pads		
6 Bag of dry snacks		
7 Travel-size wipes/tissues/hand sanitizer/lip balm		
8 Chewing gum/Ear plugs (to relieve air pressure during flight take off and landing)		
9 1 set extra clothes (in case luggage gets lost or misplaced)		
10		
11		
12		
13		
14		
B. LUGGAGE/CHECK-IN BAGGAGE		
1 Season-appropriate clothes		
2 Swimwear for summer		
3 Jacket/sweater for winter		
4 Pouch for toiletries: comb, toothbrush, toothpaste, shampoo		
5 Blankie (if needed)		
6 Sleepwear, underwear, socks		
7 Shoes (_____ pairs), flip flops		
8 1 set semi-formal attire if planning to go for formal dinner/show		
9		
10		
11		
12		
13		
14		
TOTAL NUMBER OF PIECES OF LUGGAGE FOR CHILD/TEEN 2		

(Make additional copies for extra child/teen)

EXTRA FEATURE 4

PARENT/S, GUARDIAN, ADULT (1) PACKING LIST

ITEM/S		Check before departure from	
		Home	Hotel
C.	**CARRY-ON**		
1	iPad/Laptop/Portable DVD/Electronic gadget etc ...		
2	Cell phone / charger		
3	Pouch for important travel documents and money (i.e. Driver's license, Passports, Visas, Traveler's checks, Credit cards)		
4	Pouch for medicines/prescriptions/vitamins/supplements		
5	Sunglasses/prescription glasses/contact lenses		
6	Camera/spare batteries/chargers		
7	Video cam/handy cam/spare batteries/chargers		
8	Music player/MP3/iPod/earphones		
9	Pouch for cosmetics, shaving kit, toiletries, toothbrush, comb, Toothpaste, shampoo, hygiene stuff etc...		
10	1 set extra clothes (in case luggage gets lost or misplaced)		
11			
D.	**LUGGAGE/CHECK-IN BAGGAGE**		
1	Season-appropriate clothes		
2	Swimwear for summer		
3	Jacket/sweater for winter		
4	Sleepwear, underwear, socks		
5	Shoes (_____ pairs), flip flops		
6	1 set semi-formal attire if planning to go for formal dinner/show		
7			
8			
E.	**WHEN TRAVELING WITH INFANTS/BABIES/TODDLERS**		
1	Diaper bag (with essentials i.e. diaper, wipes, changing pad, diaper rash cream, pacifier, etc ...)		
2	Baby food/baby formula /feeding bottles (Check with TSA re updated hand carry rules)		
3	Pre-order infant necessities for convenience 888-450-LITE or www.babiestravellite.com		
4			
5			
6			
	TOTAL NUMBER OF PIECES OF LUGGAGE FOR ADULT 1		

PARENT/S, GUARDIAN, ADULT (2) PACKING LIST

ITEM/S		Check before departure from	
		Home	Hotel
A.	**CARRY-ON**		
1	iPad/Laptop/Portable DVD/Electronic gadget etc …		
2	Cell phone / charger		
3	Pouch for important travel documents and money (i.e. Driver's license, Passports, Visas, Traveler's checks, Credit cards)		
4	Pouch for medicines/prescriptions/vitamins/supplements		
5	Sunglasses/prescription glasses/contact lenses		
6	Camera/spare batteries/chargers		
7	Video cam/handy cam/spare batteries/chargers		
8	Music player/MP3/iPod/earphones		
9	Pouch for cosmetics, shaving kit, toiletries, toothbrush, comb, Toothpaste, shampoo, hygiene stuff etc…		
10	1 set extra clothes (in case luggage gets lost or misplaced)		
11			
12			
13			
14			
B.	**LUGGAGE/CHECK-IN BAGGAGE**		
1	Season-appropriate clothes		
2	Swimwear for summer		
3	Jacket/sweater for winter		
4	Sleepwear, underwear, socks		
5	Shoes (_____ pairs), flip flops		
6	1 set semi-formal attire if planning to go for formal dinner/show		
7			
8			
9			
10			
11			
12			
13			
14			
TOTAL NUMBER OF PIECES OF LUGGAGE FOR ADULT 2			

(Make additional copies for extra child/teen)

EXTRA FEATURE 5

SAMPLE 4-5 DAY ITINERARY
LAS VEGAS GETAWAY

DAY 1 – ARRIVAL DAY

ACTIVITY	PLACE	TIME	COST *	COMMENTS
Arrival	Airport	2 hours	_____	Check how much luggage, strollers, etc.
Pick-up car	Car Rental	1 hour	_____	Check special requests: car seat, GPS navigation, maps, mobile phones, etc ...
Check in hotel	Hotel	1 hour	_____	Check special requests: non-smoking rooms, crib, extra cot, view etc ... Infant supplies online delivery.
Getting situated/ mealtime	Restaurant	2 hours	_____	Check hotel facilities/amenities, etc. Mealtime - feed baby/children.
Cruising around/getting to know the city Or start hotel-hopping.	The Strip (Las Vegas Boulevard) Downtown	1 to 2 hours	_____	For best results, drive around during the night when the city is ablaze in vibrant-colored glory. Daytime also offers a different and unique view of the city.
Free attractions: Dancing fountains, Conservatory, Chocolate falls	Bellagio Hotel	2 to 3 hours	_____	Allow at least 30 minutes to an hour for parking and walking in and out of hotels.
Atlantis show, Forum Shops Aquarium	Caesar's Palace	2 to 3 hours	_____	Food/Dining options also available in these chic places
Dinner - Rainforest Café or other locations	MGM Grand Hotel	1 hour	_____	Or other convenient dining place of your choice. Or light snacks and settle in for the night depending on arrival time

OTHER FUN STUFF/YOUR NOTES:

_____	_____	_____	_____	
_____	_____	_____	_____	
_____	_____	_____	_____	
DAY 1 TOTAL			*	

* Synchronize with Travel Budget Checklist, Extra Feature 5

LAS VEGAS GETAWAY

DAY 2

ACTIVITY	PLACE	TIME	COST *	COMMENTS
A.M. Breakfast	Hotel/fast food	1 hour	_____	Or explore other convenient dining options in the area
Summer:				
Wet' n' Wild Water Park	7055 S. Fort Apache Road	4 to 5 hours	_____	Off Strip location, call # (702) 979-1600 for ticket prices & park summer schedule
OR				
Shark Reef	Mandalay Bay	4 to 5 hours	_____	
Secret Garden & Dolphin Habitat	Mirage Hotel		_____	
Springs Preserve	# (702) 822-7700		_____	
Red Rock Canyon	# (702) 515-5350		_____	
Bonnie Springs	# (702) 875-4191		_____	
Madame Tussauds	# (702) 862-7800		_____	
Discovery Children's Museum	# (702) 382-3445		_____	
P.M. Dinner/Buffet				
Wicked Spoon	Cosmopolitan Bellagio Hotel		_____	Or seek out other restaurants of your choice
Buffet at Bellagio			_____	
Carnival	Rio Hotel	2 to 3 hours	_____	
Wynn Buffet	Wynn Hotel		_____	
Feast Buffet	Green Valley Ranch		_____	
Adult time / Show (if not too exhausted) Cirque de Soleil Shows or shows of your choice	Various locations		_____	Check out current shows or pre-book prior to travel

OTHER FUN STUFF/YOUR NOTES:

_____   _____   _____   _____

_____   _____   _____   _____

_____   _____   _____   _____

_____   _____   _____   _____

DAY 2 TOTAL   *

* Synchronize with Travel Budget Checklist, Extra Feature 5

LAS VEGAS GETAWAY

DAY 3

ACTIVITY	PLACE	TIME	COST *	COMMENTS
M. Breakfast	Hotel/fast food	1 hour	_____	Or explore other convenient dining options in the area
...venture Dome ...atosphere rides ...w York – New York roller ...aster	Circus Circus Stratosphere New York – New York Hotel	4 to 5 hours	_____	Check height restrictions for rides
...tel hopping & Attractions: ...ondola ride	Venetian	3 to 4 hours	_____	Advance reservations for Gondola ride strongly advised
...rupting Volcano	Mirage			Free nightly show, check timings
M. Dinner/Show/Family ...tertainment Choices: ...vid Copperfield ...urnament of Kings ...iss Angel(BeLIEve) ...n Rouven (Illusions) ...rry Fator Show ...acKing Show ...athan Burton ...e Mentalist ...popovich Pet Theater	MGM Grand Excalibur Luxor The Riviera Mirage Harrahs Planet Hollywood Planet Hollywood	Allow 3 to 4 hours till end of the night schedule	_____ _____ _____ _____ _____ _____	Advance reservations strongly advised. Check half-prized ticket booths for deals on some shows Take advantage of coupons, promos, discounted rates in magazines, brochures in hotels or online deals
...THER FUN STUFF/YOUR NOTES: _____ _____ _____ _____	_____ _____ _____ _____	_____ _____ _____ _____	_____ _____ _____ _____	
DAY 3 TOTAL			*	

* Synchronize with Travel Budget Checklist, Extra Feature 5

LAS VEGAS GETAWAY

DAY 4 (or Departure Day next page)

ACTIVITY	PLACE	TIME	COST *	COMMENTS
A.M. Breakfast	Hotel/fast food	1 hour	_____	Or explore other convenient dining options in the area
Outdoor activities:				
Mini Gran Prix	# (702) 259-7000	3 hours	_____	For younger kids
	Various			
Mini Golf			_____	Check out list of Mini Golf Options
Beyond Las Vegas:	Boulder City, NV			
Hoover Dam/Lake	Arizona	4 to 5	_____	
Mead	Utah	hours		Check timings/entrance fees
Grand Canyon		Whole	_____	
Zion National Park		day	_____	Check timings/entrance fees
				Check timings/entrance fees
P.M.				
Fremont Street	Downtown Las Vegas	3 to 4	_____	Free entertainment but check o
Experience		hours		Flightlinez ride # (702) 410-7999 as added activity
	Downtown Las Vegas			
First Friday		3 to 4	_____	Free art and culture event every first Friday of the month
	Opportunity Village	hours		
Winter only:				
Magical Forest		3 to 4	_____	# (702) 259-3741 for fees/timings
	Various	hours		
Show/Dinner				
Check out list from	Airlines			
3rd day		2 to 3		
Pre check-in flight online	Hotel	hours	_____	Or early night in hotel dependin on departure time next day.
Confirm check out time /Packing time		1 hour		
				Be sure to cross-check with Packing Lists (See Extra Featur 3 & 4)

OTHER FUN STUFF/YOUR NOTES:

_____	_____	_____	_____	
_____	_____	_____	_____	
_____	_____	_____	_____	
_____	_____	_____	_____	

DAY 4 TOTAL *

* Synchronize with Travel Budget Checklist, Extra Feature 5

LAS VEGAS GETAWAY

DAY 5 - Departure Day

ACTIVITY	PLACE	TIME	COST *	COMMENTS
A.M. Breakfast	Hotel/fast food	1 hour	_____	Depending on departure time
Souvenir shopping	Bonanza Gift Shop	1-2 hours	_____	# (702) 385-7359
Other last-minute shopping	Various locations	2 to 3 hours	_____	
NOON				
Check-out time unless extension granted, always check with hotel	Hotel	1 hour		Depending on departure time, luggage can be kept at Concierge for safekeeping and collected prior to departure for airport
Mealtime/Lunch	Hotel or Airport	1 to 2 hours		Check transportation options to Airport
Departure for airport	Hotel	1 hour		Cross-check pieces of luggage with Packing List (Extra Features 3 & 4)
Car Rental return	Car Rental	1 hour		Allow at least 1 hour prior to Flight check-in including filling up gas/petrol
Check-in/Boarding	Airlines	1 hour		At least 2 hours prior to Departure time. Check TSA rules on allowable items in carry on bags (i.e. baby formula/milk etc.)

OTHER FUN STUFF/YOUR NOTES:

DAY 5 TOTAL			*	

TOTAL BUDGET COST *

*** SYNCHRONIZE WITH TRAVEL BUDGET CHECKLIST (See Extra Feature 2)**

LAS VEGAS GETAWAY
Family (Name) _____ Itinerary
Travel dates: from _____ to _____

DAY _____

ACTIVITY	PLACE	TIME	COST	COMMENTS
TOTAL				

EXTRA FEATURE 6

OTHER RESOURCES: WEBSITES, GUIDEBOOKS, MAGAZINES

www.lvccva.com Las Vegas Convention & Visitors Authority official site	www.travelnevada.org or www.travelnevada.com Nevada Tourism official site
www.lasvegastourism.com Las Vegas Tourism Bureau official site	www.lasvegasnevada.gov City of Las Vegas official site
www.lvchamber.com Las Vegas Chamber of Commerce official site	www.vegas.com Vegas travel official site

Just a few websites among thousands about Las Vegas:

www.A2Zlasvegas.com
www.alllasvegastours.com
www.amazinglasvegas.com
www.bestoflasvegas.com
www.bestofvegas.com
www.bestofvegasdining.com
www.best-las-vegas-deals.com
www.cheapovegas.com
www.earlyvegas.com
www.exploringlasvegas.com/kids
www.goingtovegas.com
www.halfpriceshows.com
www,i4vegas.com
www.ieatvegas.com
www.ilovevegas.com
www.kidsinvegas.com
www.lasvegas.com
www.lasvegas-nv.com
www.lasvegasdirect.com

www.lasvegasfrees.com
www.lasvegashotels.org
www.lasvegas-how-to.com
www.lasvegashows.com
www.lasvegasweddingwebsites.com
www.off2vegas.com
www.picklasvegas.com
www.pocketvegasdeals.com
www.showtickets.com
www.todayinlv.com
www.travora.com/las-vegas/
www.vegas4visitors.com
www.vegasexperience.com
www.vegasfreebie.com
www.vegashotelspecial.com
www.vegastickets.com
www.vegasview.com
www.viator.com/las-vegas-tours
www.visitlasvegas.com

YOUR NOTES:

OTHER RESOURCES: WEBSITES, GUIDEBOOKS, MAGAZINES (Continuation)

OTHER USEFUL INFORMATION		Website/Phone number / Other useful information	
Electronic System for Travel Authorization (ESTA)		http://esta.cbp.dhs.gov	Visa Waiver program
Transportation Security Administration (TSA) - Traveler info		www.tsa.gov	866-289-9673
Student/Teacher travel deals	STA Travel USA	www.statravel.com	800-781-4040
Advance baby products order	Babies Travel Lite	Babiestravellite.com	888-450-LITE
Babysitting & Child Care	Nannies & Housekeepers USA	lasvegasnannies.com	702-451-0021
Special Needs Traveler	SATH	www.sath.org	212-447-7284
Travel Insurance	Travel Insured International	www.travelinsured.com	800-243-3174
Show Tickets	Half Price Show Tickets	tix4tonight.com	702-212-4696
Monorail	Las Vegas Monorail	Lvmonorail.com	866-466-6672
Limo Service/Airport Shuttle	Bell Trans	Bell-trans.com	800-274-7433

BOOKS/GUIDEBOOKS

AAA Spiral guide to Las Vegas: Secrets of living the good life – for less
Fodor's Las Vegas
Fodor's 25 best Las Vegas
Frommer's Irreverent Guide to Las Vegas
Frommer's Las Vegas
Frommer's Las Vegas with kids
Frommer's Portable Las Vegas for Non-gamblers
Kidding around Las Vegas, a Parent's Guide to Las Vegas by Kathy Espen
Las Vegas for Dummies by Mary Herczog
Las Vegas, Lonely Planet Publications
Las Vegas (Main contributor, David Stratton)
The Everything Family Guide to Las Vegas by Jason Rich
The Unofficial Guide to Las Vegas

FREE MAGAZINES	TRAVEL WEBSITES
www.247vegas.com	www.expedia.com
www.insiderlv.com	www.frommers.com
www.lasvegas.net/showbiz-weekly	www.hotwire.com
www.lasvegasmagazine.com	www.kayak.com
www.lasvegasmagazine.com/vegas2go	www.orbitz.com
www.lasvegasweekly.com	www.priceline.com
www.parentsguidelv.com	www.thelonelyplanet.com
www.vegasmagazine.com	www.travelocity.com
www.whats-on.com	www.tripadvisor.com

MY TRAVEL BRAG BOOK

(Your picture here)

VISIT FROM ___ TO ___

Day 1 Fun Happenings

say cheese! ▸▸▸▸ **LOOKIN' GOOD!**

Day 2 Fun Happenings

Perfection

make the most of every day.

Day 3 Fun Happenings

Day 4 Fun Happenings

Oh Happy Day!

your pictures here

Day 5 Fun Happenings

Other Fun Adventures :-)

Other Fun Adventures :-)

memories

CPSIA information can be obtained at www.ICGtesting.com
Printed in the USA
BVOW10*1305120814

362114BV00001BA/1/P

9 781478 700210